PRESENTED TO:

_____

FROM:

_____

DATE:

_____

Jesus calling®

FOR TEENS

50 DEVOTIONS TO GROW IN YOUR FAITH

Sarah Young

Adapted by Tama Fortner

Edited by Kris Bearss

THOMAS NELSON
Since 1798

Jesus Calling: 50 Devotions to Grow in Your Faith

© 2017 by Sarah Young

Published in Nashville, Tennessee, by Tommy Nelson. Tommy Nelson is an imprint of Thomas Nelson. Thomas Nelson is a registered trademark of HarperCollins Christian Publishing, Inc.

Tommy Nelson titles may be purchased in bulk for educational, business, fund-raising, or sales promotional use. For information, please email SpecialMarkets@ThomasNelson.com.

ISBN 978-1-4003-2440-8 (eBook)
ISBN 978-1-4003-2439-2 (HC)

Library of Congress Cataloging-in-Publication Data

Fortner, Tama, 1969–
Jesus calling: 365 devotions for kids / Sarah Young; adapted by Tama Fortner; edited by Kris Bearss.
p. cm.
ISBN 978–1–4003–1634–2 (hardcover)
1. Devotional calendars—Juvenile literature. I. Young, Sarah, 1946–II. Bearss, Kris. III. Young, Sarah, 1946–Jesus calling. IV. Title.
BV4870.F67 2010
242'.62—dc22   2010017099

Printed in India

24 25 26 REP 6 5 4

INTRODUCTION

J esus calls us to trust Him at all times. Trust Him in all circumstances. Trust Him with all our heart.

Scripture says, "Trust in the Lord with all your heart, and do not lean on your own understanding" (Proverbs 3:5 ESV). The Bible is the only perfect Word of God—without errors. I work hard to keep my devotional writings consistent with the unchanging truths of God's Word.

I have written from the perspective of Jesus speaking, to help readers feel more personally connected with Him. So the first person singular ("I," "Me," "My," "Mine") always refers to Jesus; "you" refers to you, the reader. I've included Scripture references after each reading. Words from the Scriptures (some paraphrased, some quoted) are indicated in italics.

The devotions in this book are meant to help you trust Jesus more and more. When you're tired, when things are going wrong, and even on your best days, whisper these four short words: "I trust You, Jesus." When you do this, you release things into His control. This is a great way to stay close to Him and grow in your faith.

Sarah Young

DON'T WORSHIP
YOUR WORRIES

Worship your worries? That sounds crazy, doesn't it? But whatever you think about the most becomes your god, your idol, the thing you worship. When your worries take on a life of their own and take over your thoughts, you are worshiping your worries.

I want you to break free from your worries. How? By trusting Me. By thinking about Me. By worshiping only Me. No one else knows what goes on inside your mind—not your friends, not your teachers, not even your parents. But *I* know your every thought, so be careful concerning what you choose to think about. I am constantly searching your thoughts for a sign of your trust in Me. When I find that your thoughts are about Me, I rejoice! Choose to think about Me more and more; this will keep you close to Me.

1 CORINTHIANS 13:11

He is

SAFE

because he

TRUSTS

the Lord.

—Psalm 112:7 (icb)

A NEW YOU

I came to earth, was crucified, and then rose from the grave so that I could create a *new you*. A "you" who isn't stuck in a boring routine, who doesn't worry what others think, who isn't afraid to try new things.

I want you to have an exciting life, full of adventure and challenge. I have lots of plans for you; I want you to do great things for My kingdom. First, though, you have to give Me control of your old life. Let Me have your old worries, your old struggles, your old temptations and sins. I will throw them all away so that I can work in your life.

Change can be frightening, but trust Me. I have great plans for this day—and every day—of your life.

MATTHEW 28:5−7

Therefore, if

ANYONE

is in Christ,

he is a new

CREATION;

the old has

gone, the

NEW

has come!

—2 Corinthians 5:17

I WILL FILL YOUR LIFE WITH RICHES

Worship Me, and I will fill your life with glorious riches.

The world tells you that riches are money, cars, designer clothes, and beautiful jewelry. The world says grab them and hold on tight; store up these treasures for yourself.

But My riches are the far better treasures of Joy, Love, and Peace. And instead of storing them up only for yourself, I want you to share them. When you share My riches, they multiply—so that you and those around you are richer than ever before.

How can you get My riches? Worship Me! Come to Me in the quietness of morning. Praise Me for the beauty of a new day. Sing to Me of My holiness. Open your heart to Me, and let Me flood your soul with My riches.

1 PETER 1:8

Give unto the

Lord the

GLORY due

to His name;

WORSHIP the Lord

in the beauty

of HOLINESS.

—Psalm 29:2 (nkjv)

ONE OF *MY* DAYS

It has been one of those days when anything that could possibly go wrong, does go wrong. When it's been "one of those days," look for Me. Because when everything goes wrong, that is when I am working the hardest in your life. I take frustrations and turn them into opportunities to strengthen your faith. I take disappointments and turn them into chances to draw closer to Me. I take troubles and turn them into opportunities to trust Me.

Do you trust Me enough to let Me lead you through the days when everything goes wrong? Or are you determined to fix it all yourself? If you keep trying to make things go *your* way while I am leading you in a different way, you make your desires an idol. Instead of doing this, cast all your troubles and worries on Me. Then I will turn "one of those days" into one of *My* days!

1 PETER 5:6; 1 THESSALONIANS 5:18

Cast all your

ANXIETY

on him

because he

CARES

for you.

—1 Peter 5:7

PUZZLE PIECES

I gave you an amazing mind. With it you can think great thoughts and dream great dreams. But My Mind is infinitely bigger and more amazing. My thoughts contain all of creation and the universe, all of the past, present, and future. And because I understand all things and all times, My thoughts and My ways are different from yours.

Life can be like a box of puzzle pieces—with the box top missing. When you look around at your life, all you can see are the pieces. But I see the final picture. I know how all the pieces fit together. I know how to join together all the jagged pieces of hurts and disappointments, plus the smooth pieces of victories and joys.

Trust My timing and My ways. Trust Me to fit all your pieces together into a wonderful life. And trust Me—at the end of your life—to lead you home to heaven.

Isaiah 55:8; Psalm 73:23–24

For as the HEAVENS

are higher than the

earth, so are My ways

HIGHER than your ways,

and My thoughts

than your thoughts.

—Isaiah 55:9 (NKJV)

Some trust in chariots and some in horses, but we trust in the name of the Lord our God.

—Psalm 20:7

SEE MY GREATNESS

Let Me surround you with My Presence. I am King of kings and Lord of lords. When you come close to Me, I come even closer to you. You may feel overwhelmed by My Power and Glory. You may feel small compared to My Greatness. These feelings are actually a form of worship. You are telling Me that you know how powerful and wonderful I am.

Some people do not like My Greatness. They don't like feeling small compared to *anything*—not even Me. They want to be in complete control, and they want to be the most important. They may even be so wrapped up in themselves that they don't see Me at all.

Don't fall into that trap. Enjoy being in the presence of My Greatness. Be glad that you have such a great and all-powerful God who loves you and is taking care of you.

1 TIMOTHY 6:15–16; JAMES 4:8;
ACTS 17:28; PSALM 145:4–6

GREAT is the

LORD and most

WORTHY of praise;

his greatness no

one can FATHOM.

—PSALM 145:3

THE GIFT OF YOUR TIME

Don't rush through our time together. When you are in a hurry, your mind flips back and forth between Me and the things you are about to do. You have My full attention; I want your full attention too.

Set aside a special time every day just to be with Me. It can be early in the morning or just before you go to sleep. It can be soon after you get home from school. But don't let other things crowd out our time together. Then look for a quiet place where you can relax in My Presence. Perhaps it's a cozy spot in the den, or in your room. Or maybe it's outside under a tree. Find a peaceful place for us to meet. Look forward to our time together!

When you bring Me the gift of your time, I strengthen you and prepare you for what is ahead of you—this day and all your days.

PSALM 119:27; HEBREWS 13:15

For the EYES

of the LORD range

throughout

the earth to

STRENGTHEN

those whose

hearts are fully

COMMITTED to him.

—2 CHRONICLES 16:9

HOLY GROUND

At the burning bush, Moses stood on holy ground and heard the very voice of God. And now I am asking you to step onto holy ground and listen to Me!

You don't need a miraculous bush. Just leave behind the cares of this world. For a little while, forget that list of things you're supposed to get done, and just be with Me.

Don't let the world make you feel guilty for our time together. Don't listen to the lie that says you should be busy doing something more productive, something that matters. There is nothing that matters more than spending time with Me—your Lord and Savior. Block out all the noise of the world and be still in My Presence. When you do, you are standing on holy ground.

ISAIAH 9:6; ZECHARIAH 9:9; ROMANS 8:15–16

"Do not come any

CLOSER," God said.

"Take off your sandals,

for the PLACE where

you are standing

is HOLY ground."

—Exodus 3:5

WORSHIP ONLY ME

Only I am God. Only I deserve your worship. Do not devote yourself, your time, or your attention to the things of this world. Do not let them become idols, false gods.

The worship of idols has always been a trap for My people. The ancient Israelites bowed down to carved images and golden statues. But today's idols are harder to spot. They can be other people, possessions, popularity, or success. An idol can be anything that keeps you away from Me.

Don't bow down to the idols of this world. They have no real power. They can't forgive your sins, love you unconditionally, or take you home to heaven. Only I can do those things. So worship only Me. And be ready to receive Joy and Peace in My loving Presence.

EXODUS 20:5; 2 SAMUEL 22:29

You must not make for

YOURSELF an idol of

any kind or an image

of anything in the

HEAVENS or on the

earth or in the sea.

—Exodus 20:4 (NLT)

THE BEAUTY
OF CREATION

The whole of creation declares that I am God. And the beauty of creation declares My Glory.

Open your eyes to the beauty all around you. See the majesty of the mountains, the power of the ocean waves, the details of the tiniest wildflower, the endless colors of the sunset—and know that I am holy God.

So many people rush past these signs of My Presence without even giving them a second thought. Some people just use beauty to sell their products—forgetting all about Me. But I want you to open your eyes to the glory of My creation. Let this awesome beauty draw you into worshiping Me.

Be glad that I am a holy God who created such a beautiful world. And use the glory of My creation to tell others about Me. The whole earth is full of My shining beauty—*My Glory!*

PSALM 29:2

Holy, holy, holy

is the LORD

ALMIGHTY;

the whole earth is

full of his GLORY.

—ISAIAH 6:3

God is the one who saves me.
I trust him. I am not afraid.
The Lord, the Lord, gives me
strength and makes me sing.
He has saved me.

—Isaiah 12:2 (ICB)

THE GIFT OF YOUR TIME

†his world is obsessed with action. Action heroes, action movies, action adventures. You have to be busy. You have to be on the go—all the time. There is no time to just sit and be still. At least, that's what the world tells you.

But when you come to Me, you are *not* just sitting and being still. You are doing the most important thing of all—letting Me be Lord of your life. As you spend time with Me, My blessings flow over you like streams of living water. I give you blessings of Peace, Love—and the sheer Joy of being in My Presence.

I—your Lord and God—am also blessed by our time together. So bring Me the gift of your time.

JOHN 7:38; PSALM 103:11

You always

gave him

BLESSINGS.

You made him

glad because you

were WITH him.

—PSALM 21:6 (ICB)

THE WHYS AND HOWS

You want to understand everything. Why the sky is blue, how your mind works, why bad things happen, and why boys and girls act the way they do. You think if you can understand the whys and hows of things, you can control them—and then you'll have peace. But the problem is that as soon as you figure out one set of things, another set pops up for you to figure out. If you count on your own understanding to give you peace, then you will never really be peaceful.

Instead of searching for the whys and hows, search for *Me*. My Presence and My Peace go together, so when you find Me you also find My Peace.

Put your faith in Me, not in your ability to figure everything out. Besides, I already have everything all figured out.

PROVERBS 3:5–6; 2 THESSALONIANS 3:16

Therefore, since we have been MADE right in God's sight by FAITH, we have peace with God because of what JESUS CHRIST our Lord has done for us.

—Romans 5:1 (nlt)

TAKE A BREAK
FROM JUDGING

You can get into a habit of judging. You judge this situation and that situation, this person and that person. You judge yourself. You even judge the weather. So much of your time is spent making judgments—as if that were your main job in life. Actually, your main job is to worship Me. So forget about judging, and just come to Me.

I am the Creator, and you are My creation. I am the Shepherd, and you are My sheep. I am the Potter, and you are My clay. Let Me have My way in your life. It is not your place to judge—not even yourself. Judging is *My* job.

Worship Me as the King of all kings—the King who loved you enough to die for you and save you from judgment.

JOHN 17:3; ROMANS 9:20−21; 1 TIMOTHY 6:15

Do not

JUDGE,

or you

too will be

JUDGED.

—Matthew 7:1

YOUR SECRET MISSION

*S*acrifice is a difficult word to understand. And it is even more difficult to practice. It means giving up what you want for yourself in order to please or help someone else. In your relationship with Me, it means giving up control of your life—to let Me show you the way *I* want you to live. When you sacrifice your own will to Mine, seeking to please Me, that is worship.

I know that you want to be off on a great adventure for Me. But sometimes the greatest adventures are the ones you don't see. While your daily life may seem routine, your spiritual life can be involved in a huge, secret mission—to climb the mountain of trust and find the treasure of My Presence. When you live close to Me, you are offering yourself to Me as a living sacrifice. This pleases Me and helps Me turn your routine days into spiritual adventures of worship.

GENESIS 2:7; PSALM 89:15; ROMANS 12:2

Since God has shown us great MERCY, I beg you to offer your lives as a living sacrifice to him. Your OFFERING must be only for God and pleasing to him. This is the SPIRITUAL way for you to worship.

—Romans 12:1 (ICB)

WORKING FOR ME

Every day you are faced with choice after choice. When you're trying to make decisions, you need a good goal to guide you. So seek to please Me in all your choices—in all that you do.

You know that in order to please Me you need to spend time with Me. Worship, prayer, praise, and Bible study—these are things that make Me smile.

But pleasing Me isn't just about the things you do with Me. It's also about the things you do for Me. From the big things like helping the sick, giving to the poor, and being a friend to the friendless, to the everyday things like emptying the dishwasher for your mom, taking out the trash for your dad, and being respectful—do everything for Me. It may seem like you are working for others, but you are really working for Me. So do the best you can, knowing I'll be with you in all of it.

MATTHEW 6:33; JOHN 8:29; COLOSSIANS 3:24

Work WILLINGLY

at whatever you do,

as though you were

WORKING for the Lord

rather than for people.

—COLOSSIANS 3:23 (NLT)

"My sheep listen to
my voice; I know them,
and they follow me."

—John 10:27

COME TO ME

I am the all-powerful King of kings and Lord of lords—which means I have the Power to take care of you. Not only do I have the Power, but I *want* to take care of you. Will you let Me?

Some people are afraid to come to Me when they're hurting or tired. They're afraid that I will ask even more of them, when they've already worked so hard they can barely move. All of this makes them want to hide from Me.

What I want is to be their *hiding place*—and yours. Let Me heal your hurts and give you a quiet place for your soul to rest. Come to Me, and I will give you rest.

ISAIAH 55:8–9; REVELATION 2:4;
MATTHEW 11:28

The glorious God is

the only RULER, the

King of kings and Lord

of lords. . . . God will

be HONORED, and his

power will last forever.

—1 TIMOTHY 6:15–16 (CEV)

PEOPLE-PLEASERS

Don't be a people-pleaser. People-pleasers let their lives be ruled by what other people think. *I have to wear these clothes so they'll hang out with me. I can't sit with those kids—everyone will think I'm a loser. I don't want to try that stuff, but if I don't, I won't fit in.*

You can end up in scary or even dangerous situations trying to please others. Other people aren't perfect. They don't have perfect judgment, and they don't always want what is best for you. Besides, you can't really know what they truly think of you. So being a people-pleaser is foolish.

Live to please Me instead. Only I am perfect and only I care about you perfectly. Don't look at yourself through the eyes of other people, or treat their opinions as being more important than Mine. See yourself through *My* eyes—and you will see a child of God who is deeply and perfectly loved.

JOHN 4:23–24

Without faith no

one can PLEASE God.

Anyone who comes

to God must BELIEVE

that he is real and that

he rewards those who

truly want to FIND him.

—Hebrews 11:6 (icb)

BE REAL

It saddens Me to watch My children build up walls between themselves and the people around them. They pretend they don't have the same struggles and problems as everyone else.

It even happens at church. You put on your Sunday clothes and your Sunday smiles. Then you tell everyone you are just fine, while inside you are full of fear and worry and loneliness. But you don't dare to say that because—*What would people think?*

The best way to tear down these walls is to focus on My Presence with you. Talk to Me, worship Me, delight in Me—and you will feel safe enough to be *real* with others. When your main focus is on Me, you can stop worrying about what people think. Then you will be able to smile at others with My Joy and love them with My Love.

1 John 1:5–7; Exodus 33:14;

Philippians 4:8

Keep putting into PRACTICE all you learned and received from me— everything you HEARD from me and saw me doing. Then the God of PEACE will be with you.

—PHILIPPIANS 4:9 (NLT)

REFLECTING ME

See My beauty all around you: in nature, in true friendship, in love. I am the great Artist and all true beauty is a reflection of Me.

I am working to make you more and more beautiful. Bit by bit, I'm clearing out the clutter inside you—the clutter of stuff, of selfishness, of the world. This makes room for My Spirit to take charge of your life. Help Me in this work by letting go of anything I choose to take away. Whether I leave you with a lot or a little, just trust Me. I know what you truly need. And I promise to give you that—abundantly!

PSALM 29:2

I **ASK** only one thing from the Lord. This is what I want: Let me **LIVE** in the Lord's house all my life. Let me see the Lord's **BEAUTY**. Let me look around in his Temple.

—Psalm 27:4 (icb)

MAKING THE GRADE

There are so many things you get graded on. There are report cards for school and points for sports. There are scores for talent shows and beauty contests. And in a few years, you'll even be tested on your driving. Almost everywhere you go, you are graded on how well you perform.

But I don't keep score. Not ever. And I don't grade you on your performance. There is no heavenly grade book that says: Prayer Time—B, Kindness—A-, Patience—C+.

So change your focus from your performance to My loving Presence. The Light of My Love shines on you always—no matter how well you're doing or how you feel. You don't need to worry about making the grade. Because you are My child, it's A+ all the way!

EPHESIANS 3:16–19; PSALM 62:8

For it is by GRACE

you have been saved,

through FAITH—and this

not from yourselves,

it is the GIFT of God—

not by works, so that

no one can boast.

—Ephesians 2:8–9

the righteous cry out, and the LORD hears them; he delivers them from all their troubles. the LORD is close to the brokenhearted and saves those who are crushed in spirit.

—Psalm 34:17–18

PRINCE OF PEACE

I have many names: Wonderful Counselor, Mighty God, Ever-lasting Father, Prince of Peace, King of kings and Lord of lords. But in this messed-up world, it is perhaps as Prince of Peace that you need Me most.

Because I never leave your side, My Peace is always with you. You need this Peace each moment to live out My plan for your life. Sometimes you may want to take shortcuts—to reach your goal as quickly as possible. But if taking the shortcut means you turn your back on My peaceful Presence, then don't do it. Keep walking with Me along paths of Peace—even in this crazy world.

JOHN 20:19–21; PSALM 25:4

And he will be called

WONDERFUL Counselor,

MIGHTY God,

EVERLASTING Father,

Prince of Peace.

—Isaiah 9:6

DO AS THE WISE MEN DID

Come and sit with Me for a while. I want you to think about who I really am.

I am the only Son of God. I was born completely human and yet I am completely God—all at the same time. This is a mystery that is beyond your understanding. Rather than trying to figure it out, do as the wise men did. They followed a spectacular star, and then they fell down in humble worship when they found Me.

Praise and worship are the best responses to the wonder of who I am. Sing praises to My holy Name. Gaze at Me in silent worship. Look for a "star" of guidance in your own life, and be ready to follow wherever I lead you. I am the Light from heaven that shines upon you—to guide you along the path of Peace.

LUKE 1:35; JOHN 1:14;
MATTHEW 2:9; LUKE 1:78−79

When they saw the star,

they **REJOICED** with

exceedingly great joy.

And when they had

come into the house,

they saw the young

Child with Mary his

mother, and fell down

and **WORSHIPED** Him.

—MATTHEW 2:10–11 (NKJV)

A SMALL SACRIFICE

My thoughts are not your thoughts, and your ways are not My ways. Just as the heavens are higher than the earth, so are My ways and thoughts higher than yours.

When you come to spend time with Me, remember who I really am. I am the King of kings and Lord of lords! Never stop being amazed at being able to talk with the King of the entire universe—anytime, anyplace.

As you spend time in My Presence, I am training you to think My thoughts. My Spirit goes to work inside you. Sometimes He speaks to you through certain Bible verses. And other times He allows you to hear Me "speak" into your mind. Either way, this training strengthens you and prepares you for whatever you will face.

Take time to listen to My voice. Give Me this small sacrifice of your time, and I will bless you far more than you could ever imagine.

ISAIAH 55:8–9; PSALM 116:17

DEVOTE yourselves

to prayer with an

alert mind and a

THANKFUL heart.

—Colossians 4:2 (NLT)

A PRAYER I
LOVE TO ANSWER

When Jacob ran away from his angry brother, Esau, he went to sleep on a stone pillow in a land that seemed empty and gloomy. But he dreamed about heaven and angels and promises of My Presence. And when he awoke, he thought, "Surely the Lord is in this place, and I was not aware of it."

Jacob's discovery was not only for himself, but for everyone who seeks Me. I am everywhere. I am above you, below you, and all around you. There is no place that I am not. So if you find yourself feeling distant from Me, say: "Surely the Lord is in this place!" Then ask Me to open the eyes of your heart so that you can "see" My Presence. This is a prayer I love to answer!

PSALM 31:20; GENESIS 28:11–15

When Jacob

AWOKE

from his sleep,

he thought, "Surely

the Lord is in this

PLACE, and I was

not aware of it."

—Genesis 28:16

BOTH GOD AND MAN

I am the King of kings and Lord of lords. I am also your Shepherd, your Companion, and your Friend—the One who *never* lets go of your hand.

Worship Me in My holy Majesty. Come close to Me, and rest in My Presence. You need Me as both God and Man. Even though I am God, I had to come into this world as a baby and grow into the Man who became your Savior. That's the only way I could meet your biggest need—to be saved from your sins.

Since I was willing to give up all of heaven for you, and to die a terrible death for you—then you can be sure I will give you everything you need. So trust Me as your Savior, Lord, and Friend. Rejoice in everything I have done for you, and My Light will shine through you into the world.

1 TIMOTHY 6:15–16;
ROMANS 8:32; 2 PETER 1:19

Come, let us

BOW DOWN

in worship, let

us kneel before the

LORD our MAKER; for

he is our God.

—PSALM 95:6–7

And my God will meet all your needs according to his glorious riches in Christ Jesus.

—Philippians 4:19

COUNT ON ME

No one is perfect—not your best friend, not your mom or your dad, not your sports hero or favorite television star. Sooner or later, someone in your life— someone you really counted on—will let you down. You can end up feeling angry, hurt, and betrayed. You may feel like you are falling, with no one to catch you or help you up. So who can you count on?

Count on Me. I will never let you down. And when others do let you down, I will be your safety net. I will not let you crash. Not only am I always there with you, but I am holding your hand. And I promise, I won't ever let go.

PSALM 73:23—26

The LORD

your God is

WITH you,

he is mighty

to SAVE.

—ZEPHANIAH 3:17

YOU ARE SAFE

You are mine for all time—beyond time and into eternity. I will never let go of your hand. And nothing can take you out of My hand. You are completely safe with Me.

Because you know that your future is secure, you can live fully today. Don't see today as a blank page that you need to fill up. Live it! I have lovingly and carefully planned this day for you. I have paid attention to every detail—big and small. Be on the lookout for all that I am doing. Talk to Me throughout the day. Ask Me to show you the wonders of this day. It sounds easy, but to do it, you have to trust Me deeply. Trust that you are safe, and that My way is the perfect way.

PSALM 37:23–24

The **WAYS** of God

are without fault. The

Lord's words are **PURE**.

He is a shield to those

who **TRUST** him.

—Psalm 18:30 (icb)

AND THAT IS FAITH . . .

I am nearer than you think. I am present in every moment in your life. Nothing can *ever* separate you from Me.

But I know that sometimes you still feel alone. Even though My Presence is there with you, you don't feel it. Ask Me to open your eyes so that you can "see" Me all around you. I am in the hug of a parent and the smile of a friend. I am in the beauty of a sunset and the majesty of mountains. I am in that soft whisper in the back of your mind that says you are important and loved.

The more you sense My Presence around you, the safer you will feel. I am far more Real than this world that you can see, hear, and touch. And that is faith— knowing and trusting in My Presence as a real fact even though you can't see Me with your eyes.

ACTS 17:27–28

70

FAITH makes

us sure of what

we hope for and

gives us **PROOF** of

what we cannot see.

—HEBREWS 11:1 (CEV)

DON'T PRACTICE YOUR PROBLEMS

Everywhere you go, I go. Nothing can separate you from My Love. I love you so much that I even gave My Life for you. You can trust Me to take care of you.

Sometimes, though, when you aren't really focusing on Me, you start to rehearse and practice your problems—going over them again and again in your mind. What will you do about that grade, this friendship, or that temptation? You start to feel alone and worried. Then you try to fix it yourself.

But you are *never* alone, because My Presence goes with you wherever you go. There is no need to worry, and you don't have to fix anything by yourself. Bring your problems to Me. In My Presence, many problems simply vanish, and others become much easier to handle.

Don't practice your problems; practice bringing your problems to Me.

ROMANS 8:38–39

The Lord replied,

"My PRESENCE

will go with you,

and I will give

you REST."

—Exodus 33:14

ROCK-SOLID

This world is constantly changing—time passes, seasons change, people change. Even your body is constantly changing and growing. Nothing on this earth stays the same. But *I* never change. I am always the same—yesterday, today, and forever.

Because I never change, you can always count on Me. Friends may move away; you may switch churches or schools; homes can be destroyed. Sometimes it can feel like your life has been turned completely upside down. When that happens, come to Me. I am rock-solid. You never have to be afraid, because I am always with you and I never change.

REVELATION 1:8; HEBREWS 13:8; PSALM 48:14

Long ago you laid the

FOUNDATION of the earth

and made the heavens

with your hands. They will

perish, but you remain

FOREVER; they will wear

out like old clothing. . . .

But you are always the

same; you will live forever.

—PSALM 102:25–27 (NLT)

Being afraid of people can get you into trouble. But if you trust the Lord, you will be safe.

—Proverbs 29:25 (ICB)

SHOUT IT OUT LOUD

The devil is like a playground bully. He likes to push around those who are feeling weak. He will shove you with a lie, telling you that you're not good enough. He'll attack you with your secret fears, and kick you when you're down.

When you start to feel lonely or afraid or worthless, call out My Name. Tell Me you trust Me. Speak out loud, if you are in a place where you can do that. If not, even a whisper will do. The devil will know that you are not alone—that I am by your side, fighting for you. And then, like the cowardly bully that he is, he will run away.

Chase him away with songs and prayers of praise. Strengthen yourself with My promises—I am always with you; you can do all things with My help; you are My own special creation. Stay close to Me, because the devil will be back—and together we will chase him away again.

ROMANS 8:1–2; ISAIAH 12:2

SUBMIT yourselves,

then, to God.

RESIST the devil,

and he will

FLEE from you.

—JAMES 4:7

I SET YOU FREE

I did not come to this earth to make you feel guilty. I came to free you from guilt.

And I don't like it when others use guilt to get you to follow Me. I want you to come to Me out of love— because you want to be in My Presence.

It is true. I know every mistake you have ever made, every sin you have ever done. But when you come into My Presence, I don't see your sins; I see My beloved child. When you ask Me to forgive you, My grace washes all your sins completely away. Not only do I forgive them, but I forget all about them. I set you free.

ISAIAH 61:10; ROMANS 8:1; PSALM 103:11–12

I am not JUDGED guilty

because in Christ Jesus

the law of the SPIRIT

that brings life made

me free. It made me

FREE from the law that

brings sin and death.

—ROMANS 8:2 (ICB)

I PROMISE YOU

I am always here for you.

Once you have trusted Me as your Savior, I never leave your side. There may be times when you feel far away from Me. But that is just a feeling; it is *not* fact. You can find the truth in My promises throughout the Bible. I promised Jacob that I would never leave him. I promised Joshua the same thing. And My last promise was to all of My followers: I am with you always, until the end of time. I promised them, and I promise you.

The mountains may disappear and the hills may come to an end, but even then I will never leave you. My Love lasts forever; it never fails.

GENESIS 28:15; JOSHUA 1:5; MATTHEW 28:20

"The mountains may disappear, and the hills may come to an end.

But my LOVE will never disappear. My promise of peace will not come to an end," says the Lord who shows MERCY to you.

—Isaiah 54:10 (ICB)

FAITH IS KNOWING

Every moment of every day, I am working for your good. So bring Me all your worries and fear. Talk with Me about everything. Let the Light of My Presence chase your shadows away.

Bring Me your hopes and dreams too. Let's work on them together, changing them little by little from wishes to reality.

All this takes time. Don't try to take shortcuts or rush the process. When you work with Me, you must learn to accept My timing. Remember how long Abraham and Sarah waited for a son? But when Isaac finally came, their joy was even greater because of their long wait.

Faith is *knowing* I will keep My promises— believing that things you are hoping for are as real as things you can already see.

GENESIS 21:1–7

For with

you is the

FOUNTAIN

of life;

in your light

we see LIGHT.

—Psalm 36:9

YOUR AMAZING MIND

I created you in My own image. You are the best of My creation. I gave you a mind that is capable of amazing, creative thoughts. And I risked everything by giving you the freedom to think for yourself. Your wonderful human mind makes you totally different from animals and robots.

I could have created you so that you *had* to always love Me and seek Me. But I wanted you to use your mind to *choose* loving and seeking Me.

Your mind is amazing. It can imagine, it can dream, and it can also rebel. Bring your mind and thoughts to Me. Let Me take away the anger, the doubts, the rebellion—and give you Love, Faith, and Peace.

GENESIS 1:26; ROMANS 8:6

So God **CREATED** man in his own image, in the **IMAGE** of God he created him; male and female he created them.

—Genesis 1:27

those who know your name
will trust in you, for you,
LORD, have never forsaken
those who seek you.

—Psalm 9:10

YOU ARE SAFE WITH ME

You are completely safe and secure in My Presence—even when you don't feel that way. You are never separated from Me because I never leave you.

When you forget that I am with you, you may feel lonely or afraid. If that happens, say a prayer or whisper My Name: "Jesus." This will remind you that I am still right beside you. As you focus on Me, I will replace your loneliness and fear with My Peace.

As wonderful as My Peace is now, it is nothing compared to heaven. In heaven I will still be right by your side, but you will be able to *see* Me. You and I will talk face-to-Face. And your Joy will be bigger and better than anything you can imagine!

1 CORINTHIANS 13:12

The LORD gives

STRENGTH

to his people;

the LORD

BLESSES

his people

with **PEACE.**

—PSALM 29:11

TAKE A BREAK WITH ME

ake a break. Put aside your to-do list. For a little while, put aside your chores, your practices, your playing, and even your homework. Stop trying to figure everything out, and hang out with Me. I created you to need rest. Not just the kind of rest that comes from sleeping, but the kind that comes only from spending time with Me—rest for your soul.

Ask Me to take charge of the details of your life. Remember that you are on a journey with Me. When you try to look into the future and plan for everything that might happen, you ignore your Friend who is with you all the time. While you're worrying about what's up ahead, you don't even feel the strong grip of My hand holding yours. How foolish that is, My child!

Never lose sight of My Presence with you. This will keep you resting in Me every day.

1 THESSALONIANS 5:17

Find REST,

O my soul,

in God alone;

my HOPE

comes from him.

—PSALM 62:5

THINK THE THOUGHT

You've heard people say "Walk the walk." This means you should live the way you know is right. Well, now I am asking you to "think the thought." Think the way you know you should—with thoughts centered on Me. When you do, there is no room for thoughts of sin, revenge, hatred, self-pity, or gossip.

I know sometimes a thought just zips into your brain—you don't know where it came from and you don't want it there. Toss it right back out again. I don't hold you responsible for that kind of thought. But when you find yourself holding on to a bad thought—or returning to it over and over again like a familiar song—then you need to bring that thought to Me. Don't try to hide it. Confess it and leave it with Me. Then you can go on your way with a clear mind and a forgiven heart.

PSALM 20:7; LUKE 1:79

But if we

CONFESS

our sins,

he will

FORGIVE

our sins.

—1 John 1:9 (ICB)

STICKS AND STONES

The saying, "Sticks and stones may break my bones, but words will never hurt me," just simply isn't true. Words can cut deeper than any knife. And the wounds they leave behind may never heal.

The world praises people who say "clever" things—even if they embarrass and hurt others. But that is *not* the kind of person I want you to be. Your words are powerful tools. I want you to use them to build up those around you, not tear them down.

I know you get angry and frustrated at times, but don't say the first thing that pops into your mind. Pray first! Before you pick up the phone, pray. Before you answer someone else's angry words, pray. Before you say *anything*, pray! A simple, split-second prayer—"Help me, Jesus"—is all it takes to put your words under My control.

PROVERBS 12:18; JAMES 1:19

When you TALK, do

not say harmful things.

But say what people

need—words that will

help others become

STRONGER. Then what

you say will help those

who listen to you.

—Ephesians 4:29 (ICB)

I AM YOUR BEST DEFENSE

When you sit quietly with Me, trusting Me, it may look like you are doing nothing. But you are really at war. There are great and terrible battles being fought every day in spiritual realms, and your quiet trust makes a difference.

By quietly trusting in Me, you are using some of heaven's greatest weapons. This battle is not fought with guns, tanks, or rockets. This battle is fought with spiritual weapons. The evil one uses fear, loneliness, anger, and shame to attack you. But My weapons are more powerful. Fear is defeated by trust. Loneliness is cast out by My Presence. Anger is erased by My Peace. And shame is driven away by forgiveness. Stay close to Me—I am your best defense against evil.

JOHN 14:27; ISAIAH 30:15

We **FIGHT** with weapons that are different from those the world uses. Our weapons have **POWER** from God. These weapons can destroy the enemy's strong places.

—2 Corinthians 10:4 (ICB)

those who hope in the LORD will renew their strength. they will soar on wings like eagles; they will run and not grow weary, they will walk and not be faint.

—Isaiah 40:31

SHAKE IT OFF

I have a perfect plan for your life. So trust Me and try to see things from My point of view. When things don't go quite the way you expected, shake them off. Look up at Me, shrug your shoulders, and say with a grin, "Oh, well." Then just let them go—and move on.

This simple act of trust will keep you from weighing yourself down with little frustrations. With enough practice, you will discover that most of the things you worry about just aren't that important. Your energy and time won't be wasted on things that really don't matter—and you'll have the strength to deal with big problems when they do come your way.

You know that thing that's bothering you right now? Shake it off, and let's move on together.

2 CORINTHIANS 4:17–18

The LORD

DIRECTS

our steps,

so why try to

UNDERSTAND

everything

along the way?

—PROVERBS 20:24 (NLT)

UNCONDITIONALLY

Remember that the devil is the father of lies. He likes to sneak into your thoughts and whisper lies to you. One of his favorites is to tell you that I don't really love you *unconditionally*. Satan wants you to believe that you have to be good enough to be loved. If you make one little mistake—if you even think about a sin—then surely I won't love you anymore.

That is a lie. I love you, *no matter what*. This world is full of temptations. It's hard to always resist, and it's impossible for you to be perfect. I understand that. I walked on this earth, too, and I was exactly your age once.

But be encouraged: I lived a perfect life in this world and then died to wash away your sins. And I rose from the grave to be your Savior. All because I love you—*unconditionally*. Come close to Me, and I'll wrap you up in My perfect Love.

Ephesians 3:16–19; Hebrews 4:14, 16;
John 8:44; James 4:7–8

Jesus UNDERSTANDS

every weakness of ours,

because he was tempted

in EVERY way that we

are. But he did not sin!

—Hebrews 4:15 (cev)

DON'T DIVIDE
UP YOUR LIFE

I want you to learn to trust Me in all things. Not just the big things, and not just the things you know you need help with. *All* things.

Don't divide up your life into what you can do by yourself and what you need My help with. Don't say to yourself, "I've got my weekend figured out, but I'll let Jesus figure out my life." Or, "I can handle this argument with my friend, but I need Jesus' help with this big trouble at home."

Train your mind to constantly seek My help and My way—in every situation. Even when you are sure you know the right thing to do, double-check with Me. The more you trust Me, the more you will be able to enjoy life and face each day with confidence.

PSALM 37:4–6; PHILIPPIANS 4:19

TRUST

in the

LORD

and do

GOOD.

—PSALM 37:3

YOU ARE VALUABLE

Worry is the result of imagining a future without Me in it. So your best defense against worry is to stay in contact with Me—both talking to Me and listening to Me.

Sometimes you do have to think about the future. The key is *how* you think about it. If you only think about the things *you* must do to plan and be prepared, then you will start to worry.

So when you must plan ahead, follow these two rules: First, don't spend very much time thinking about the future. The more you think about it, the easier it is to start worrying. And second, always include Me in your thoughts. Don't just imagine what you will do—imagine what *I* will do.

You can trust Me to take care of you—today *and* in the future. Remember how very valuable you are to Me!

Luke 12:22–23, 25–26; Ephesians 3:20–21

CONSIDER the ravens:

They do not sow or

reap, they have no

storeroom or barn; yet

God **FEEDS** them. And

how much more valuable

you are than birds!

—Luke 12:24

WHO I AM

I am God with you. You hear about this so often in church. But don't ever let it become ordinary. Don't ever stop living in awe of Me.

Stop and think for a moment about who I am. My Name is Jesus. It means "the Lord saves." I save you. I save you from the troubles and despair of this world. And I save you from your sins for all eternity.

I am also Immanuel, which means "God with us." *God with you.* I am always with you, and I'm always waiting to hear from you. Tell me about whatever makes you happy, whatever upsets you, whatever is on your mind.

Don't ever get so used to Me that you forget the wonder of who I am or the Joy of knowing Me—the God and Creator of all the universe.

MATTHEW 1:23; ACTS 2:28

She will give

birth to a SON,

and you are to

give him the

name Jesus,

because he will

SAVE his people

from their sins.

—Matthew 1:21

Jesus replied, "Didn't I tell you that if you had faith, you would see the glory of God?"

—John 11:40 (CEV)

I AM FOREVER

I am with you and for you. You never have to face anything alone—ever! When you are worried, you are thinking about the things of this world—the things you can see—and you are forgetting about Me. It is easy to be distracted by what you can see, but those things are only temporary. And even though you cannot see Me, I am forever.

Getting rid of your worries is simple: Keep your thoughts on Me. Whisper My Name to remind you that I'm with you. Sing a song of praise. Tell Me that you trust Me. I will get you safely through this day and every day.

This day is a precious gift. Don't waste it worrying about the future. Instead, unwrap the gift of today and enjoy its many blessings with Me by your side. As you open this today-gift fully, you'll find Me!

2 CORINTHIANS 4:18; GENESIS 16:13–14

What, then,

shall we say in

RESPONSE to this?

If God is for us, who

can be against us?

—ROMANS 8:31

THE FUTURE
IS MY SECRET

Sometimes you think it might be nice to know the future, what to expect, how things will turn out. There are even some people who claim they can tell you the future. But the future is a secret. It is *My* secret.

When you try to figure out the future, you are reaching for something that is Mine. By keeping your future a secret, I am teaching you to depend on Me. Trust My promises to care for you, to look out for you. I will show you the next step you need to take, and the one after that, and the one after that—one step at a time. Don't try to rush ahead of Me. Just relax and enjoy the journey to your future—one day at a time.

Psalm 32:8

There are

SOME things

the Lord our

God has kept

SECRET.

—Deuteronomy 29:29 (icb)

JUMP IN WITH BOTH FEET

You will never be in complete control of your life. It just isn't possible. You want to feel completely safe and secure. But even if you plan out every detail, the world will mess up your plans.

So just stop trying to be in control. Stop trying to make your life completely safe and predictable—*and boring*! Instead, grab My hand and jump in with both feet. I am the One who loves you completely and wants only the very best for you. I want your life to be an amazing adventure—filled with new things. But first you have to let go of old ways of doing things. Then, grab hold of My hand, and look for all the exciting *new* things I've prepared for you!

Romans 8:38–39; Psalm 56:3–4

Look at the NEW thing I am going to do. It is already happening. Don't you see it? I will MAKE a road in the desert. I will make rivers in the dry land.

—ISAIAH 43:19 (ICB)

IT'S NOT A SUGGESTION

Do not worry about tomorrow! This is a command, not a suggestion. I divided time into days for a reason—to make your life easier.

When you pick up the worries of tomorrow and carry them around today, it just makes today harder. And it doesn't help tomorrow at all. Sometimes you carry around the worries of next week, next month, or even next year! You stumble and stagger under the weight of worries that I never meant for you to carry.

Don't just let go of your worries—get rid of them entirely by bringing them to Me. Then concentrate on My Presence with you today. I will give you all that you need, taking care of you—and helping with your problems—today. Then tomorrow, I will do it all over again. *Trust Me.*

MATTHEW 6:34; 2 CORINTHIANS 12:9

TRUST God all

the time. Tell

him all your

problems.

God is our

PROTECTION.

—Psalm 62:8 (icb)

I ALREADY KNOW

I am God. I am here, there, and everywhere. All at the same time.

I am God. I am yesterday, today, and tomorrow. All at the same time.

That is how I am able to take care of you completely. I get up with you in the morning, *and* I am already waiting for you on the bus. I eat lunch with you, *and* I already know what you will have for dinner. I go to sleep with you each night, *and* I already know where you will be fifty years from now.

So when I tell you not to worry—that I will take care of you—I mean it! I know what problems you will face tomorrow. I've already seen them, and today I'm preparing you to face them. So leave tomorrow's worries where they belong: in tomorrow. And when you *do* get to tomorrow, I'll already be there—without ever having left your side today.

JOHN 10:10; JAMES 4:13–15

So don't **WORRY**

about tomorrow, for

tomorrow will bring

its own worries.

TODAY'S trouble is

enough for today.

—MATTHEW 6:34 (NLT)

When I am afraid, I will trust in
you. In God, whose word I praise, in
God I trust; I will not be afraid.
What can mortal man do to me?
—Psalm 56:3–4